YOU CAN PRAY!

Meditations for Teens

NORA BROWNE

Scepter

Published by Scepter Publishers, Inc.
info@scepterpublishers.org
www.scepterpublishers.org
800-322-8773
New York

ISBN: 978-1-59417-184-0

May you seek Christ, may you find Christ, may you love Christ.

—ST. JOSEMARÍA ESCRIVÁ

CONTENTS

INTRODUCTION

I KNOW IT CAN BE HARD TO PRAY at times because even though you know you are speaking with God, you may wonder, is he really listening? I can assure you he is extremely interested in everything you say and in everything you ask for.

I became very aware of this recently when I was having some trouble at work, and I didn't know what to do. I just put the whole issue into God's hands and asked him to sort it out for me because I just couldn't do it myself. I said to him very plainly, "Please sort this problem out for me because I don't know what to do," and that was it. No long prayers, just a simple plea, in my own simple words. I was actually astounded when, a few days later, the problem sorted itself out, and has not returned since. So have faith—God wants us to ask him for things, and although that is not the only kind of prayer there is, it is a good place to start.

To pray is really quite easy: we just need to realize that God is near and that he is ready to listen to us whenever we want to talk to him.

However, at times this can take a bit of effort; we may have decided to pray and nothing occurs to us, or we don't know how to start or what to talk about. If you find yourself in that situation, this little book may help you to begin. It might give you some ideas about how to talk to God, your Father in heaven.

I hope that this book helps you to pray. Not just to pray using prayers from a prayer book, or saying the prayers you learned when you were younger (although it is good to say them daily), but to pray by talking to our Lord, using your own words, talking to him about the things that are in your mind and that matter to you.

USING THIS BOOK

The way to use this book is to read each point slowly, think about it, and see how it applies to you and your situation, and whether it suggests to you any improvements you can make in your everyday life or your spiritual life. If you find yourself thinking, "Well, yes, I do that," or "No, I don't do that," or "Sometimes I behave like that," you can talk this over with our Lord and ask for his help to improve in one way or another.

The first step is to begin well, and this means making a good act of faith—to tell God that you know he is there. You could say something like "O my God I really believe you are here with me. Help me to pray well." The best place to pray is in a church, in front of Jesus in the tabernacle. But if you can't go there, then any place will do (as long as it is quiet and you'll be reasonably free of interruptions and distractions), because God sees and hears us always and everywhere.

When you have decided what you want to pray about, picture Jesus right next to you, happy to listen to what you have to say and eager also to talk to you. It's not just your imagination; he really is! But don't expect to hear his voice. Usually he speaks to us just by putting good thoughts and ideas into our minds.

KEEPING IN TOUCH WITH GOD

01 When Jesus was on earth, many people went to him to ask his advice. One of these people was a man called Nicodemus who came to Jesus by night, as we read in St. John's Gospel. Nicodemus opened his heart to our Lord and told him all his hopes and fears. Jesus spoke words of wisdom and goodness to him, and he went away thoughtful and at peace.

We too can talk with Jesus often, every day, and we too will come away thoughtful and at peace.

02 Lord, you spent time talking to Nicodemus, helping him to understand the mysteries of God. I too want to learn the value of conversation with you, so make me ready to listen as Nicodemus was. Help me to be ready and willing to listen to what you say because I know that it is what you want for me. Teach me to want to do your will.

03 You may have never thought about how good it is to pray. Maybe it just reminds you of going to church, or of the days in religion class when you may have been told to join your hands and close your eyes.

> *Jesus, help me to see that you want me to pray, that you want me to talk to you, and that you and I can "chat" at any time of day, in any place, and about anything I want.*

04 We tend to take so much for granted, and to feel we have a right to so many things. One of our greatest gifts from God is our guardian angel, but we hardly think of him at all, and so we do not ask him for help, when he could be such a support. But from now on we will remember our guardian angel every day, and we will thank him for all the favors he does for us, and all the protection he gives us, even though we are quite unaware of it.

05 You might complain that you pray for things and don't get them, and so you think there's no point at all in praying. Well, to start with, prayer is not just a matter of asking for things. Secondly, God does listen to you and answer prayers, although sometimes the answer might be "No" because what you are asking for would not be good for you. Or God might simply be saying "Not yet," because he wants you to pray a bit harder or for a longer time to see if you are really convinced about what you want. If you are the type of person who stops praying because you don't immediately get what you think you should get, then you are acting a bit like a spoiled child who has a tantrum whenever he is told "No." Would you give in to a spoiled child? So, keep going and don't give up praying. God is listening and you will receive what is best.

06 Aspirations are short sentences, a few words that we say to God or to our Lady or St. Joseph or some other saint. You can say aspirations during the day as you go up or down a staircase, as you open or close doors, as you walk along the street. It is a wonderful way of being close to God, and since you say them in your heart, nobody else notices that you are praying, only God and whoever else you are saying them to.

07 Aspirations are a great help for staying aware of God's presence, and they can also be a good support for us in trying to live our Christian life well. Try to get into the habit of saying many each day.

08 If we say aspirations to our Lady, she will help us in our spiritual lives. She will, in other words, help us be close to her son, Jesus.

Holy Mary, our refuge and strength, pray for us.
Immaculate Heart of Mary, help us in our needs.

09 Try not to forget your prayers, even when you're very tired. Say them before you get into bed. Otherwise there's the danger that you will fall asleep and leave them out altogether.

Jesus, I will find a few moments to pray every evening;
help me not to give up on that too easily.

10 It is very good to say vocal prayers—the Our Father, the Hail Mary, etc.—but make sure you say them well, with your heart as well as with your lips.

11 You say you don't see any need for prayer—it's for children and old people—and anyway you don't know how to pray. Well, don't you talk to your friends about all sorts of things, important and not? If you share your thoughts with your friends, then if you try, you can share your thoughts with our Lord because he's your best friend.

12 In order to say your morning prayers you may need to get up a few minutes earlier to fit them in. But what is losing a few minutes in bed when there will be the whole of eternity—in heaven!—to rest if you want to; though you probably won't want to, or need to.

WANTING TO SHINE
Getting Things in Perspective

13 Most if not all of us have the desire to be really good at something; we want to reach our greatest potential in our chosen sport or in our academic classes. We would so like to shine! But do we have the same eagerness to reach our full potential in our knowledge and love of God? Are we aiming to shine here as well?

14 God has given us so many gifts; the gift of life, to start with, and then everything else to go with that. He has given us intelligence, willpower, and physical gifts to use to the best of our ability. Perhaps up till now we were thinking that our life was in our hands, and that we were in complete control of it. It may not have occurred to us that our life comes from God, not ourselves, and that it is he who holds us in existence. From now on we can thank God many times a day for all that we have even when we feel that things are going against us and that life is unfair.

15 Jesus loves us very much all the time, but especially when we go to him ready to turn over a new leaf, when we are ready and willing to be a better person.

Lord, I want to do this, but I need your help.

16 Strive always to set a good example, realizing that when others see us behaving badly, they can be led to do wrong by our bad example.

Lord, I will always try to do what is right. I don't want to be a show-off, trying to look big in front of my friends.

17 There are many really poor people around. If you know that you probably will not often go hungry or be without proper clothing or a bed to sleep on, you should be very grateful. And see if you can do a little something to help the ones who are really hurting. Praying for others who are less fortunate is pleasing to God. Maybe once in a while you could also donate your allowance to a local food bank to help those who are hungry, or donate clothes that you've grown out of.

Jesus, you are very good to me. Thank you for making sure that I have what I need. I promise to try not to grumble or complain when I don't get what I want, and to try to help you take care of the poor.

18 God has thought of us from all eternity. He loves us for ourselves, as unique individuals. But he wants us to be holy; he wants us to love him back—and to love him in loving others. How are we trying to be close to him? Do we try to put him first?

Think of what St. Augustine said: "You made us for yourself, and our hearts are restless until they rest in you."

19 I hear someone saying "I don't like the sound of 'being holy,' because it makes me think of someone praying all day and looking pious." Is that you? Well, this is not the type of holiness I am talking about. Being holy for you means praying, yes, but it also means working hard, enjoying yourself, thinking about others, being a good and loyal friend, using your time well, and going to the sacraments.

20 Think: Do I complain about every little pain? Do I give up when I have something difficult to do? Do I put my own comfort ahead of the needs of others? Do I give in to the temptation to lie, or give in to laziness?

But don't just think about these things; ask our Lord to help you make some resolutions that will help you overcome these faults in order to help you grow in holiness—in love of God and neighbor.

SHOWING LOVE FOR GOD

21 Do you remember that it is our Lord who is in the tabernacle? Do you ask God to help you have more faith in this reality?

Lord, help me to always make a good genuflection in front of the tabernacle to show that I believe you are there.

22 To genuflect well in front of our Lord in the tabernacle shows that you have love and faith in Jesus hidden there. Lord, help me to believe in you more.

23 Our Lord Jesus Christ is hidden there in the tabernacle, waiting for you and me to go and talk to him. Let's try not to pass by a Catholic church without going in, even if it's just to say "hello," because our best friend is there.

24 Jesus is really there, hidden in the tabernacle, under the appearance of bread. So try not to ignore him. Say to him slowly, "Lord, I firmly believe that you are here, that you see me, that you hear me. I adore you and love you with all my heart. I am sorry for all those people who do not know you and who do not love you."

25 Whenever you do have to pass by a Catholic church, say a little prayer silently to our Lord hidden in the tabernacle. And if you can't think of what to say, just say "I love you, Jesus."

26 Try to pop into a Catholic church whenever you can to say a prayer to our Lord, who perhaps hasn't had any visitors that day. He will be ever so grateful for that bit of attention you pay him. And try to take a friend with you as well.

27 Our Lord said, "If you love me, you will keep my commandments" (John 14:15). When we really love someone we do all we can to avoid hurting them and we try to do what pleases them. If we want to love God, we should try to avoid sin, which is the thing that really offends him.

28 The Ten Commandments are not just a set of rules laid down for us whether we like it or not, but signposts which keep us on the road to heaven. How would you manage to get anywhere on a road or highway that had no signs to direct you? Well, how do you think we will get to heaven without the signposts of the Ten Commandments to guide us in how to live?

29 When you consider the Ten Commandments you may think of God as someone who wants to stop you from having fun. But that is not true. In fact, he loves you a great deal and it isn't that he doesn't want you to enjoy yourself; he wants you to avoid anything that could take you away from him, which is a completely different thing. And sin is precisely the thing that takes us away from him.

Lord, help me to be true to you.

30 We might find the Ten Commandments difficult to accept but through them God is calling our attention to the fact that we have to love him above all things, and everyone else for his sake. By following Christ's example in this, we will live fulfilling and happy lives.

31 Say often to Jesus: Lord, I don't know you enough and I don't love you as I should. Help me to get to know you better. Help me to love you more.

GETTING TO KNOW GOD MORE

32 We all need to grow in our knowledge of God and in the truths of the faith. So try to make as much effort in learning about the faith as you do in learning about science, computers, music, fashion, sports. You can't really appreciate what you don't know, and you won't appreciate the beauty of the faith unless you know it well. What you learned in grade school is not going to be enough to answer all the doubts or problems that may arise in later life. Keep improving in your knowledge of the faith by reading and perhaps by taking classes on the faith. It will help you a lot.

33 One of the greatest enemies of God is ignorance— people don't know the one true God, and instead they run after any old thing that seems to be in fashion at the time. Let's decide here and now to discover the true God and real, everlasting happiness will be ours.

Lord, I promise I will get to know you better.

34 Get to know the Catholic faith very well by reading the Catechism of the Catholic Church and other good books on the faith. It will help you make the right decisions, and you'll be firm in your convictions. You will also be able to explain to your friends why you believe what you believe.

35 Many people don't know the meaning or purpose of life. We have to show them what it is by the example of our love of God and the practice of our faith.

36 You may sometimes find yourself in a tug-of-war between wanting to please yourself and wanting to please God. A battle, for instance, over whether to stay in bed or get up for Mass. Try always to put God first, and then you will see how, in a funny sort of way, you will be a much happier person for not having given in to your laziness, and for having been generous toward God.

37 Nowadays many people want to shut God out of their lives by saying he does not exist and then trying to forget him. But at the same time, deep down, they want to get to heaven (where in fact God is). Doesn't this attitude seem a little strange? Do you ever find yourself having it?

38 Our Lord would like to have a lot of really loyal friends. Let's decide to be good friends with him: to love him, talk to him, be loyal to him.

39 You might be thinking heaven is very far away and "why shouldn't I wait until I'm really old to think about death?" But heaven is not as far away as you imagine, and you never know when God will call you. Don't wait for tomorrow to love God; start today.

MAKING UP WITH GOD

40 God never abandons us, no matter how bad we have been. It's we who abandon him. We turn our backs on him when we are so indifferent to him, and when we give in to sin.

Lord, may I never deliberately commit any sins and turn my back on your love.

41 Don't be afraid of going to Jesus, even when you have sinned. He is always ready to forgive. Being afraid of going to him would be like being afraid of going to the doctor when you have injured yourself or gotten sick. Don't you remember what Jesus says in the Gospel that he has come for the sick and not the healthy?

Jesus, help me to be ready to say "Sorry" and help me to want to improve my life.

42 One good way you can help yourself think of God is to say acts of contrition at various times in the day—even when you don't feel you have done anything wrong—because you will begin to realize how good God is to you and how mean you have been toward God up to now. These acts of contrition can also be used to make up for your past sins and for the wrongs others commit which they are not sorry for; and God will be very happy with this generous spirit of yours.

> *O my God, because you are so good, I am very sorry that I have sinned against you, and with the help of your grace I will try not to sin again.*

43 When someone comes and says that they are truly sorry for having upset you or hurt you, you feel much closer to them and you become better friends. Well, the same thing happens when we say acts of contrition. When we tell God we are sorry for having offended him, we come much closer to him.

> *Lord, help me to see where I have gone wrong and be sorry for it.*

44 I would advise you to do an examination of conscience every night. Make it short—one or two minutes should be enough—and try to think, in awareness of the presence of God, about what you have done that was good, what you have done that was bad, and what you could have done better. Try to make a little resolution for the next day about something you are going to do better in, and then end with an act of contrition as you go to bed, leaving everything in God's hands.

45 If a person wants to stay slim, they avoid eating certain foods, even if it's a great sacrifice. If someone wants to avoid cancer, they might stop smoking. If we want to get to heaven, we have to avoid sin—which destroys the soul as a cancer destroys the body.

Lord, may I hate sin because you hate it so much.

46 Many people today have lost what we might call "the sense of sin." They don't think sin exists anymore, and they sometimes seem to actually think they can do no wrong. This is a bit naive. When we do something wrong, when we break one of the Commandments, it does offend God, who is all good, all loving, all merciful, and by our personal sins, we turn in on ourselves and turn away from God.

47 We sometimes think we never do anything wrong. And it may be true that most of our faults are small ones, and that we haven't committed any serious sins. But all the same it is good to go regularly to confession so that we can get the grace to fight those faults.

48 Are you thinking you don't do anything wrong and therefore don't need to go to confession? Well, let's think. Have you never said something mean, been rude to your parents, told a lie, told a dirty joke, blown up at somebody just because you were in a bad mood....? These may not be very serious things, but you don't have to have committed a murder to benefit from going to confession.

49 When you and I really think about what our Lord went through during his Passion and death, it can change our lives forever.

> *Jesus, when I am weak, when I am tempted to sin, give me the grace to overcome these temptations. Help me to see that I gain nothing and lose a lot by offending you, and that I am certainly not happier when I give in and do what is wrong.*

BEING TRUE TO YOURSELF
AND LOYAL TO GOD

50 Jesus could have chosen an easy life. He could have been born into a rich family. He could have had a very high-paying job. In fact, he could have had lots of money and not needed to work at all. But he chose a very different kind of life; he wanted to serve others, not be domineering. He wasn't money-grabbing; he chose to be poor. He did this to give us an example of how to win heaven for ourselves. May we be happy to work hard, do favors for others, and spend our money carefully and wisely.

51 We don't want to appear goody-goody to our schoolmates, and so we tend to laugh at their rude jokes and use the same bad language that they do, so that we keep in with the crowd and not appear "different."

Being a good Christian probably won't separate us
from our friends. It should bring us closer to them

because by our good example and our natural way
of behaving (which will include telling good jokes),
they'll be encouraged to see Christianity as something
challenging and enjoyable.

52 Lord, I seem to have the kind of mind which remembers the hurtful things other people have done to me and I feel angry toward them.

Help me to forgive and forget so that I don't stay
mad at people.
And Jesus, anyone that I am upset with at any
given moment, help me to pray for them and try to
see the good in them because I know that you, Lord,
love them and want them to be good.

53 Having fits of anger and displaying a temper are not signs of strength, but signs of weakness and lack of self-control. Explosiveness has no benefits; it only humiliates you and others, and then puts people on guard against you.

Blessed are the meek (the patient, the kind), because
they are able to master themselves.
Ask our Lord to help you have this self-mastery,
and also the patience you need for dealing with
difficult people.

54 Many young people follow the crowd and behave badly as a result, because they don't want to be considered uncool or lame. Don't try to be like them just because you're afraid of being left out. Have enough strength of character to be an example of good and right living for your friends. They will come to admire you for it in the end.

55 Sacrifices don't necessarily have to be very big to be of value in God's eyes. Making an effort to be kind to people who are disagreeable, or to avoid gossiping and spreading stories, can be more pleasing to God than a day of fasting.

56 So, you don't want to conform? Great! Don't go along with those friends of yours who think that being anti-God and anti-authority is a sign of nonconformity and being a radical with a strong will is showing "personality." Stand up to these people when it is difficult, and show them that to love God and do his will demands personality and a (sometimes very) strong will. Be a rebel! A rebel for God.

57 Schoolwork is very important. It does not matter whether you are 'a brain' or not; struggle always to do it as well as possible, offering those hours of work to God, and you will come close to him through it.

58 Before you start your work, offer it to God; do it as well as you can, and it will become a way of helping you win a higher place in heaven and achieve the needed graces for yourself and others.

59 "I don't want God to complicate my life." Well, that's because it is easier (sometimes) to do wrong than to do good. We're inclined to do just what we want and not pay attention to what God might be asking of us. But following our own selfish ways does not bring us true happiness in the end.

Lord, help me to see that my happiness lies in doing what is right.

60 We have to learn to be generous toward other people and willing to do acts of service for them, starting at home with our brothers and sisters and our parents. Our Lord came on earth to serve, not to be served. Let's try to imitate him in this at least. Jesus will be very pleased, and we will win merit for ourselves in heaven.

61 Try to get up straight away each morning, without giving in to laziness. It won't kill you. Instead it will help to make you a better person with a strong character. You can lead others to our Lord by showing that you are able to conquer your laziness from the very first moment of the day.

OBEYING WITHOUT RESENTING

62 Does obedience mean acting like a robot, or like an animal trained to do things without thinking? Jesus obeyed, and he didn't find this humiliating. We should obey intelligently and not as though we were robots. Believe it or not, obeying willingly actually adds strength to our character, because when we do as we are asked we show that we are able to overcome the tendency to rebel, something we all have.

63 How is your obedience? Have you ever thought of actually trying to obey cheerfully, without complaining, without finding reasons why you shouldn't do what you are being asked to do?

Lord, teach me the value of a willing obedience.

64 We read in the Gospel that Jesus "did everything well" (Mark 7:37). Could you and I receive that very same compliment?

65 Do you think that obedience is only for those with weak wills and weak characters? No, it more often shows strength of character, because we have to go against our own inclinations. Let's ask our Lord to help us realize that obedience—doing what we are told—is very good. (That is, as long as what we are being told to do is in line with God's laws.)

Lord, help me to want to obey at all times.

66 It is very easy to get into bad company. Be careful with your choice of friends and keep your distance—but in a nice way—from anyone you find to be leading you away from God.

67 Do you become upset when someone contradicts you or won't do what you want? Learn to be flexible. Such a confrontation is a good opportunity. Learn to see in it something to offer our Lord. Instead of getting upset, graciously give in and let the other person have their way. Your turn will come later.

Lord, help me to be less selfish and to cheerfully let the other person have first choice.

WATCHING, READING, AND LISTENING

68 You have begun to take your Christian life seriously, and you now begin to doubt whether certain magazines you read are good for you. Ask advice from your mother, or some other good Christian. And don't be upset if you have to throw those magazines in the garbage can. Some are like poison and belong there.

69 We can spend lots of hours in front of the TV watching program after program, but if someone were to suggest that we try to spend a few minutes in prayer, then we would say that we haven't really got the time—we are so busy and have to do our homework. Are we really being truthful? Couldn't we turn the TV off for a few minutes and use that time for God? Or is it that we just can't be bothered?

Jesus, help me not waste so much time in front of the TV, and instead give some of that time to you.

70 People who produce teen magazines and programs are not usually concerned about the truth, or about giving good and proper advice. They often seem to think that all young people want to be immoral. Be discerning in what you read. Reading the wrong thing can do great harm to your soul and feed your mind with ungodly thoughts. Publications and programs aimed at young people are, for instance, often offensive to God because they promote a distorted view of sex and undermine marriage and the real beauty of committed love.

Lord, I read these magazines and watch these programs because my friends do and I don't want to feel left out. Give me the strength of character to say "NO!"

71 There are plenty of good books to read which increase your general knowledge and enrich you culturally, and which are not boring or old-fashioned. Try not to be influenced by what your friends read, because there is a lot of garbage written and these books can influence your way of thinking without you fully realizing it.

Jesus, I want to be like my friends and read the things they read; otherwise they might think I am "out of it." Well, perhaps I can be a little bit "out of it" for you. From now on I will be careful about what I read, and I'll ask about books I am not sure about.

72 A young friend of mine once asked if listening to pop music was bad. In itself, it's not bad, but sometimes the lyrics and the rhythm can lead to sensual thoughts and feelings which can be sinful.

73 Some musicians deliberately set out to corrupt people, and often they are looked up to. But when you delve into their lives, they may be filled with drugs, drunkenness, infidelity, criminal behavior, and lots of unhappiness despite all their fame and fortune. Some of these celebrities even end up committing suicide. Are these the kinds of ideals you want to live up to? Try to look to Jesus, to our Lady, and to the saints for your inspiration and ideals.

9
GOING TO MASS

74 When you go up to receive Holy Communion, try to avoid distractions. For instance, don't look around to see who is there. Instead, think about whom it is that you are going to receive, and say something to him to help you receive him more worthily. You can tell him: "I wish, Lord, to receive you with the purity, humility, and devotion with which your most holy Mother received you, with the spirit and fervor of the saints."

75 I have heard people say that they find the Mass boring. Perhaps it's because they don't put any effort into it, but just go there expecting to be entertained (or bored), and planning to leave as soon as possible. They go to Mass because they feel they have to, because they are told to, but they don't put much love into it. To some extent, what you get out of the Mass is in proportion to how much you put into it; so if you make a real effort to participate well in the Mass, it will not be boring. It will become a treasure and powerhouse of prayer.

76 You have come to see the Mass for what it is—the one sacrifice of Jesus that was made on the cross. As an old priest used to tell us at school, the Mass is Calvary all over again. A very simple but very sound statement. Calvary in a way becomes present to us there. When you go to Mass, try to imagine that you are there at the foot of the cross, next to Mary and St. John, taking in all that is going on.

> *Lord, I need you to help me see the Mass not as a chore, but time well spent in your presence, together with Mary.*

77 Don't always show up for Mass at the last minute. Try to be a couple of minutes earlier at least so that you can pray a bit and get focused before Mass starts. Use the Mass also to pray for all your intentions.

> *Jesus, help me to pay more attention to the prayers. Help me to make them my own so that I can love the Mass more.*

78 As we have said, the Mass is the renewal, the making present, of the sacrifice of Jesus on the cross. It is also a commemoration of the Last Supper, the event in which our Lord first gave us his body and blood as food and drink for our souls. Would you have said that the Last Supper or the Crucifixion was boring if you had sat next to Jesus at the Last Supper or stood beside our Lady at the foot of the cross?

10

KNOWING THE TRUTH AND BEING FREE

79 Does it ever seem like religion is all about not getting to do what you want, or about being told it is wrong or being made to feel guilty about it? Well, remember that freedom and happiness come not from doing just whatever you want or whatever you feel like doing, but from choosing what is good and right; this is what the Church keeps telling you.

God, help me to understand that I am really using my freedom when I choose to do what is good.

80 You might think that the Commandments are too demanding and take away your freedom to do what you want. But what exactly do you want to do? Steal? Cheat? Lie? Disobey? Fight? Is that how you want to use your freedom? That's really a cockeyed notion of freedom. Whenever you break any of the commandments you damage yourself and you may be stepping on somebody else's freedom. So, in fact, everyone can't always do what they want. But is it so bad?

81 Think about this: True freedom consists in choosing good and avoiding evil. Not many people realize this. Lord, I would like to understand it, and then I can help explain it to my friends. Jesus, help me to want to do what is good and pleasing to you. Always.

82 Can you truthfully say that you didn't know what you were doing was wrong? Could it be that you didn't really want to find out the truth? Look deep into your heart and see if you are trying to turn away from God and justify your bad behavior. Don't you realize that when you discover the truth, that truth will make you free?

83 Don't be afraid to get to know the truth even if that means you have to change. That change of heart and behavior may be painful, but in the end you will find it worthwhile and will discover a happiness you've never felt before.

84 God will not force himself on us. And so we can foolishly reject him because he respects our freedom. He wants us to love him freely—to love him because we want to—and he is willing, in order to safeguard that freedom, to take the risk of our going away from him. Don't you find this amazing?

*Now let's ask our Lord to give us the grace always
to choose him, to use our minds to know him, our
wills to keep close to him, our hearts to love him.*

85 If you don't know the way to where you want to go,
you can't get there unless you set about finding out—acquiring knowledge. If you want to get to heaven, you need to
find out how to get there; and Jesus and his Church are
here to guide you. Ask God to help you have more faith
in the teachings of the Church, because when we live our
faith fully, we are truly free.

86 Do you ask the Holy Spirit to help you choose to do
the right thing always and in everything?

87 Anytime you are not sure how to act, ask for guidance.
To behave badly and plead ignorance is not acceptable. It
is the Holy Spirit who makes us truly free, by prompting
us to discover what is good for us and for others. Doing
silly, foolish, or evil things is not an affirmation of freedom.
On the contrary, in doing such things we act against our
freedom, making ourselves slaves to our whims and impulses.

*Lord, help me always to be truly wise and to choose
what is good, even though I may find it difficult.*

88 We should try not to fall into the temptation of thinking that we should not believe in sin because this belief takes away our freedom, and that the Church labels things as sins in order to stop us from doing what we like and to give us a guilt complex. Sin actually makes us slaves of our selfish passions—or, perhaps, of the devil!—and our Lord came on earth precisely to free us from our disordered passions and the clutches of the evil one.

Lord, help me to really hate sin.

89 God loves your freedom. And he respects it. But he wants you to use it wisely. He wants you to use your freedom to love him, not to turn against him, which is what you do when you freely choose what is wrong.

90 God really cares for you—do you care for God?

91 If you and I really knew God, and really understood that he only wants what is good for us, how many things we would avoid—things that take us away from him!

92 Don't think that getting to know God and loving him will mean that you have to give up regular fun things like hanging out at the mall, going to the movies, and so on. These things are good so long as they don't become opportunities for you to offend God by the kind of movies you see or by the way you behave at the mall.

Jesus, help me to enjoy all these things in the right way, so that they don't take me away from you.

93 We are all very important to God; he has called each one of us by name. "I have called you by your name; you are mine," we read in the book of Isaiah. So if you ever feel that no one loves you, that no one cares about you, remind yourself that the one that counts the most—God—always loves you, and that he cares about you a lot. Go to him with love and confidence and tell him your troubles, and he will listen to you and help you.

11

BEING UNENSLAVED TO FADS, WHIMS, AND FANCIES

94 Offering little sacrifices or mortifications to God is a good way of saying to him "I love you." And it helps build up and strengthen that love, because if we can practice on things that aren't sins, then we'll find it much easier to say no to things that are, and to do greater deeds of love that may entail a bit more discomfort. It's kind of like boot camp for the soul. A good sacrifice to make at mealtimes is to eat a little more of what you don't like, and a little less of what you do like.

Lord, this seems quite a simple thing to do, but it can be a real sacrifice. And I will offer it up to you for particular intentions.

95 I once read that happiness in heaven was for those who knew how to be happy on earth. Are you really happy? Ask yourself what your happiness depends on. Are you only happy when you get what you want, when you go where you want, when you do what you want? Do you really think this is going to make you truly happy, truly satisfied?

96 Some think that happiness can only be found in the things of this world—having money, the latest style of clothes, the newest video game or smart phone, expensive vacations. Our true happiness lies in our love of God. Does God get much of your attention?

97 Some people seem to eat constantly during the day, having a snack whenever they feel like it. Now that you have decided to follow Jesus more closely, you can offer him little sacrifices throughout the day, such as not eating those potato chips till lunchtime, not having that candy bar, or drinking water instead of a soft drink ....

98 I think we all know what suffering is, and many people avoid it as much as possible. They run away from anything that is hard or difficult—they're cowards, in a way. When you have to do something that you find hard, do it cheerfully, without complaining or pouting.

99 Sufferings and pain are not good in themselves, but if we accept them the way Jesus did and the way saints did and still do—not running away but facing their pain bravely—our souls can experience a great deal of good.

100 Our Lord has offered to give us heaven if we really love him with all our heart and with all our mind. That's not a bad reward, is it?

LOVING YOUR FAMILY

101 When you have a problem or something is worrying you, talk it over with our Lord, but also take your mom or dad into your confidence as soon as possible. Although you might not think so, they do have experience in most matters, and probably have gone through the same things you are going through, and can give you good advice.

Do you try to see your parents as your best friends?

102 Chances are, your mom and dad are your best friends, in the sense that, next to God, they love and care about you the most. God has entrusted you to them for them to look after you and bring you up properly until you are ready to bear your own responsibilities. They love you and want what is best for you, even if occasionally, when they say no to you, you may not think so.

103 Try to love and respect your parents a lot even when they seem to be giving you a hard time. It is not easy to be a parent, and so you should try to make it a bit less difficult by being thoughtful and obedient.

104 Do you tend to be overly concerned about having things like the latest video game, or the most fashionable clothes? Instead, try to be content with what you have, and to make the most of it, and to be grateful to your parents for all their efforts to make sure you have what you need.

Lord, help me to be a happy and grateful person, and not to be greedy for more and more "things."

105 Be helpful at home. Overcome any tendency you may have to think that your mother should wait on you hand and foot, or that she should give you right away whatever you ask for. Couldn't you wait on her a bit more instead?

106 Don't always get into a bad mood when Mom or Dad asks you to do something in the house—to lend a hand with the dishes, or to do some cleaning, or even just to tidy up your own room. Think about it: do you ever have to remind your mom to make dinner or to wash the clothes or to do the shopping? She does it without being asked, for the love of you and the love of God. By being helpful and cooperative, you can show your love and appreciation for your parents, and this pleases God very much.

107 If you get angry when your mother tells you to be in by a certain time and you would have liked to stay out longer, then realize that this is a sign that she cares about you and doesn't want you to get into any danger being out late at night. Would you rather she let you do whatever you want and not care what happens to you?

108 St. Paul wrote, "Children, obey your parents in everything, for this pleases the Lord" (Colossians 3:20). Actually, obedience is one of the best ways you can show your love for your parents. It is a wonderful way to please God like Jesus, who was obedient "unto death, even death on a cross" (Philippians 2:8).

109 We read in the Gospel that Jesus washed the feet of his disciples. If we want to follow his example, we won't complain when we are asked to do what we might consider a menial job, like helping with the dishes, setting the table, or cleaning the bathroom. You can make any job more important by putting love of God into it.

Lord, help me to do any job well, giving glory to you by means of it.

110 Don't despise helping around the house as though it were beneath your dignity. Our Lady, who is Queen of

Heaven, spent all her life just doing housework, but how holy she became through it! It can make you holy too, if you do it with the right attitude. Give it a try!

13
LOVING YOUR MOTHER IN HEAVEN

111 Not only was our Lady generous toward God, but she spent her life doing good to others. Can the same be said of you? Are you kind and generous to others?

112 Do you say the Rosary? It is a wonderful prayer, and is very effective. Our Lady is a powerful intercessor with God—he cannot say no to her!

113 To make the Rosary more meaningful, offer each mystery for an intention, and think about the mysteries as you say them.

114 If you really love our Lady, I think you will love her Rosary. Try to say it with more love each time, and it will become much more meaningful.

115 Pope John XXIII once said that the only bad Rosary was the one that was not said. So don't worry if you find your mind wandering as you pray it. Keep going; it's not hypocrisy.

116 You feel that the Rosary is too long? Well, when you get into the habit of saying it often, it isn't that long. Maybe it's just that your love is short! Ask our Lady for a bigger heart.

117 Pray to our Lady a lot. It isn't old-fashioned, and neither does it mean we're insulting God. We're being like good children who put all their confidence in their mom while at the same time not forgetting their dad, because they know the two are inseparable.

118 You depend on your mom for a lot of things, and when you ask her for things, you presume you will get them. Well, it's the same with our Lady. You can ask her for all your needs and desires, and, having put them in her hands, you can presume you will get them if they're for your good.

119 Some people say that Catholics pray to Mary too much and make too much fuss over her, and that it's all very silly. All I can say is that if God chose her to be his mother, who are we to ignore her or slight her? Besides,

Mary has great power with God because she is perfect and God loves her very much.

Lord, give us the grace to love your mother as much as you do.

120 Yes, some people do say that the Rosary is old-fashioned, long, and boring; that one is just repeating words that have no meaning. Perhaps they have never said it properly! You, keep up the Rosary. And if at first you find it long, just say a decade or two at a time, trying to say them well, and remembering who you are talking to.

Mary, help me to say your Rosary well; help me to enjoy saying it, help me to want to say it.

14

BEING A TRUE FRIEND TO YOUR FRIENDS

121 We tend to think that when we talk to God we have to use a different language and speak with a "holy" voice. However, we can and should talk to God in the same way as we would talk to someone in our family or a good friend.

Jesus, help me to see you as a friend rather than some distant being who has no effect on my life.

122 We all want to be loved and appreciated, but how much we are, a lot of times, depends on us. If we are selfish and mean, we won't attract friends and people won't want to be in our company. We need to learn to give ourselves to others—to do favors for them, to be interested in their concerns, to listen patiently to their complaints, to be pleased when they have some success, to help them when they are worried.

Friendship is one of the greatest joys in life. A good and faithful friend is more precious than money or gold.

*Lord, I promise, from now on, to be a good friend
to my friends.*

123 It's easy to criticize and bad mouth someone who
has upset or hurt you. Before you fly into a rage, try to
find excuses for their behavior—perhaps they are worried
about something, or they have had a big disappointment,
or someone has given them a rough time. Ask our Lord
for the strength to forgive and forget.

124 When we really think about what our Lord went
through during his Passion and death, it can change our
attitude forever.

*Jesus, when I am weak, when I am tempted to sin, give
me the grace to overcome these temptations. Help
me to see that I gain nothing by offending you and
that engaging in wrongdoing will not make me happy.*

125 Sometimes you might think "Why am I here?"
The real answer is "Because God wants you here." When
God made his plans for the universe, he thought of all
the people he wanted, and out of all the possible people
he could have created at a certain time and place, you
were one of the ones he chose to create because he knew
there was going to be a part in his plan, a job that needed

doing that no one else could do as well as you. So you do matter to God; you have an important part to play in the history of the world, no matter how big or how small. Go on. Go for it!